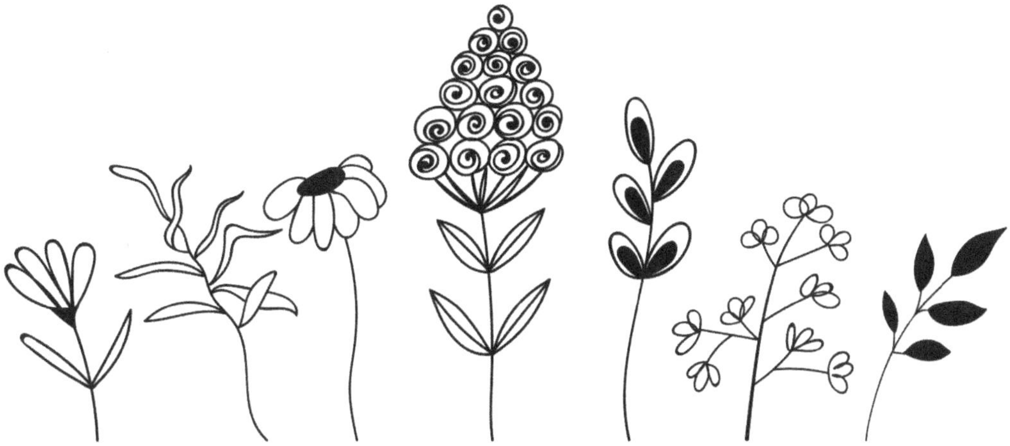

THIS JOURNEY BELONGS TO ___________

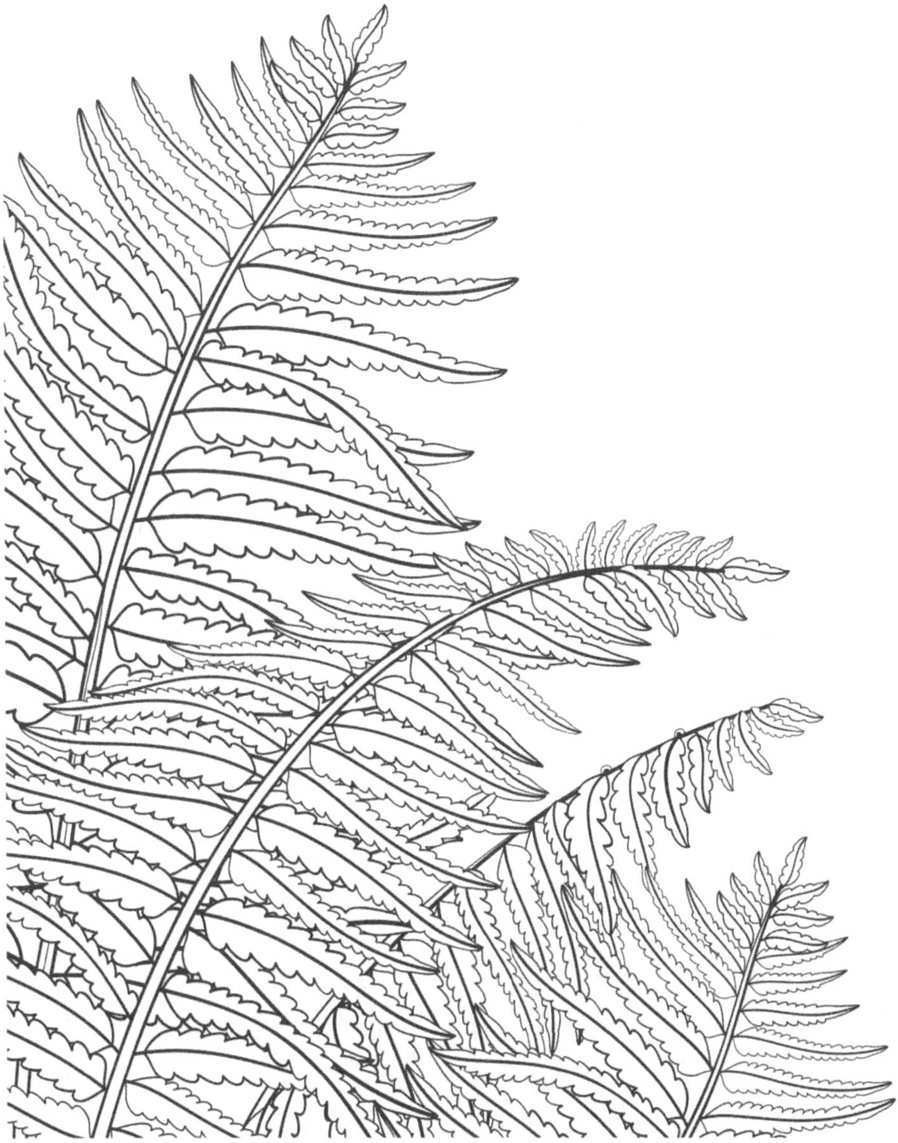

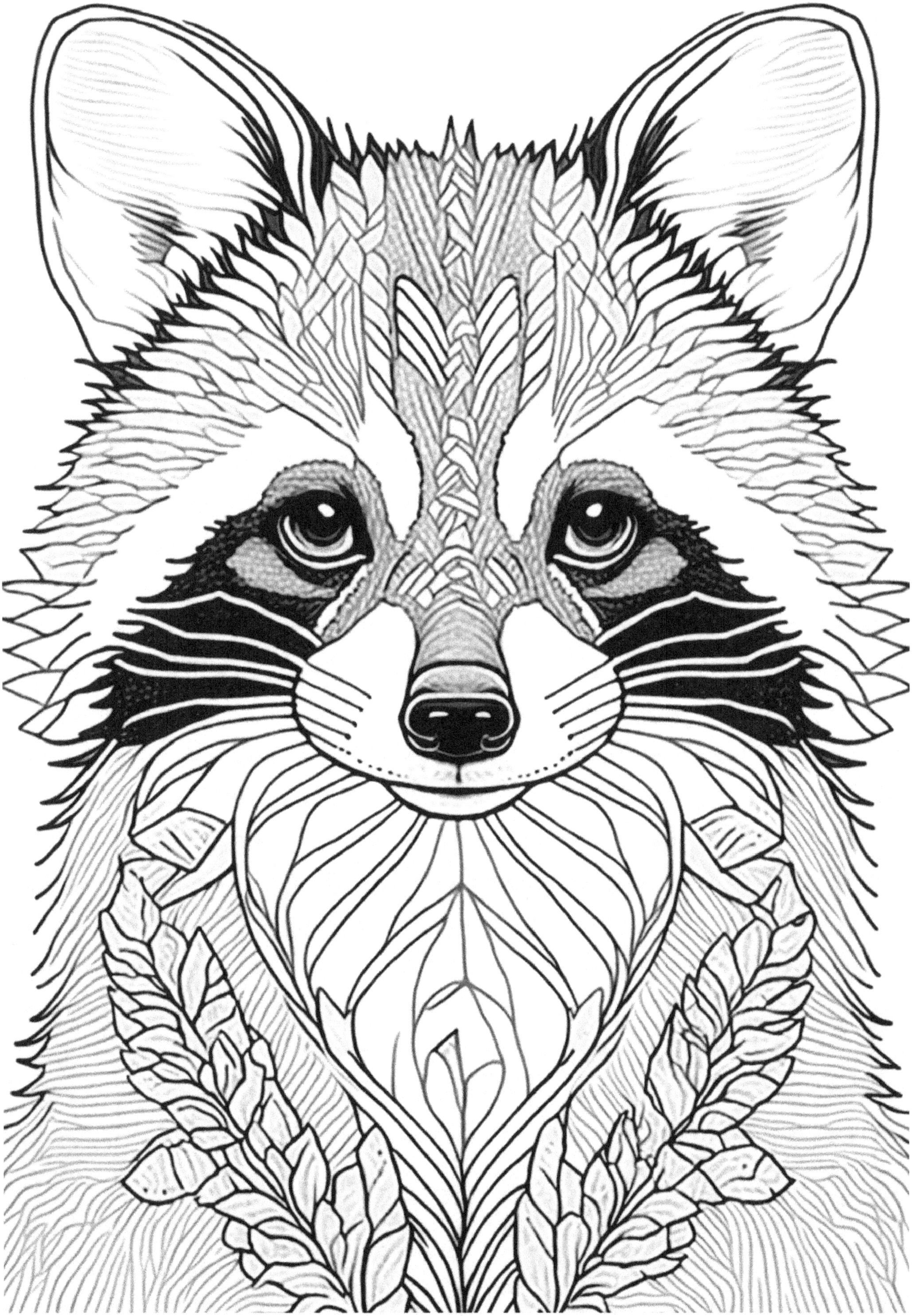

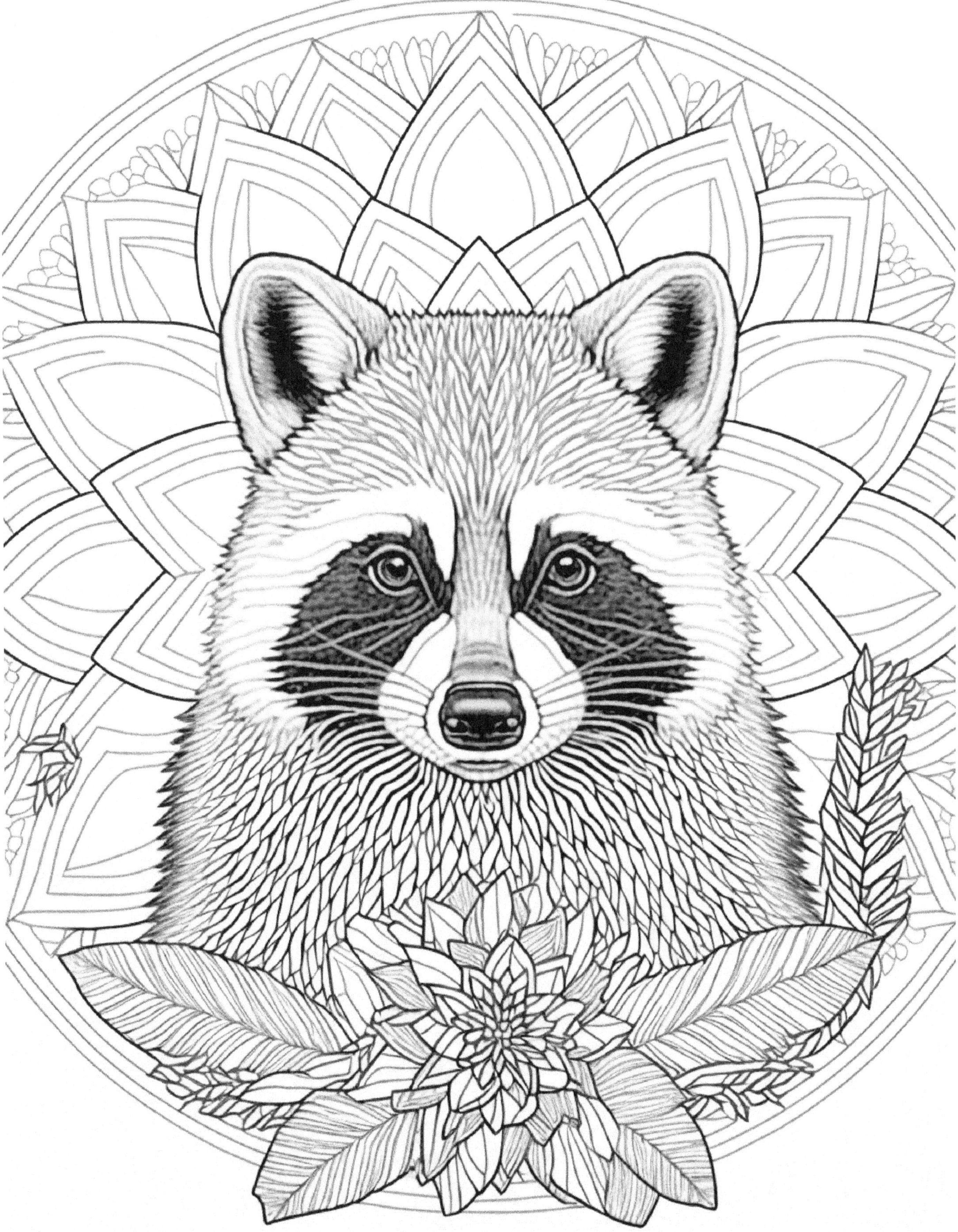

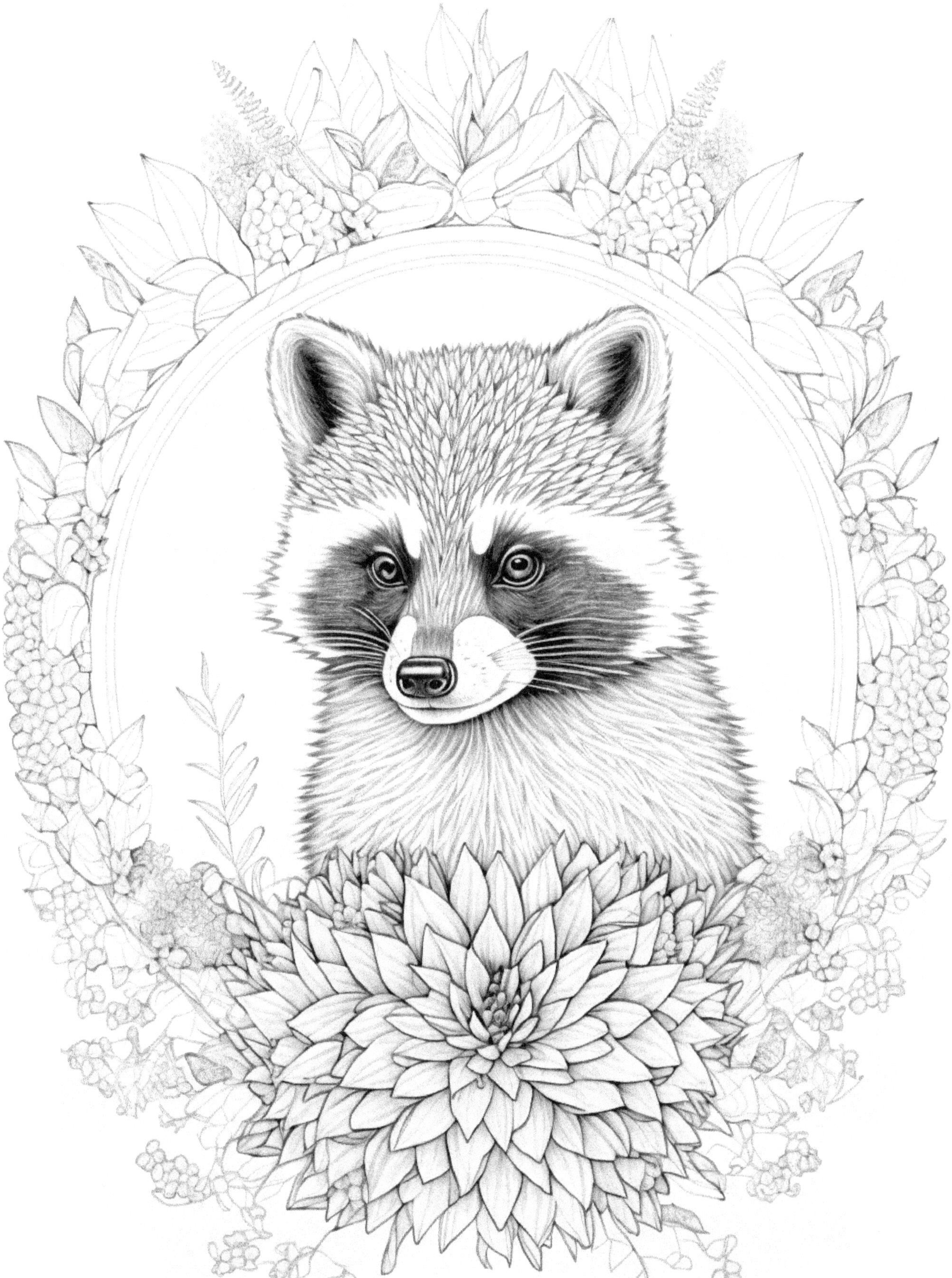

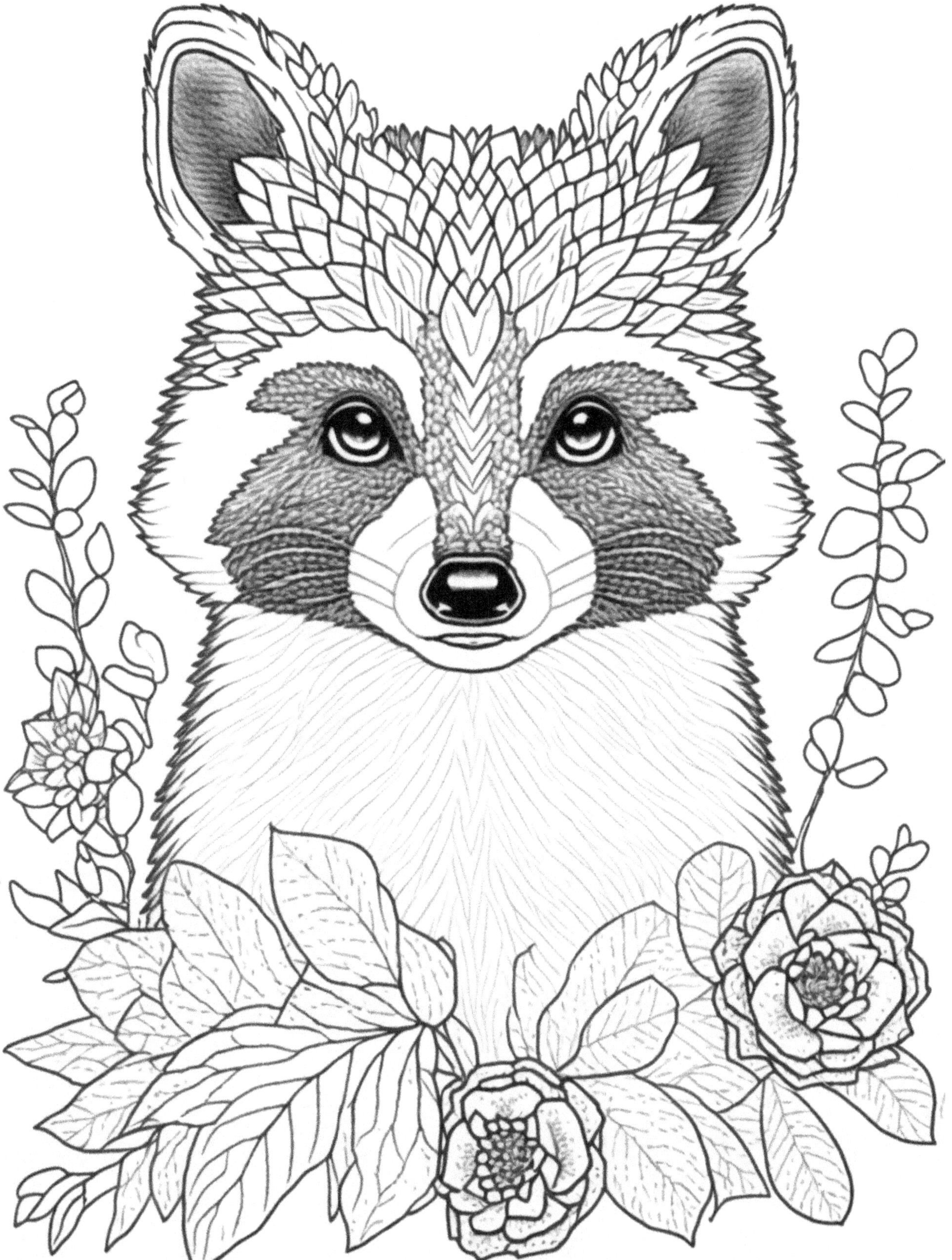

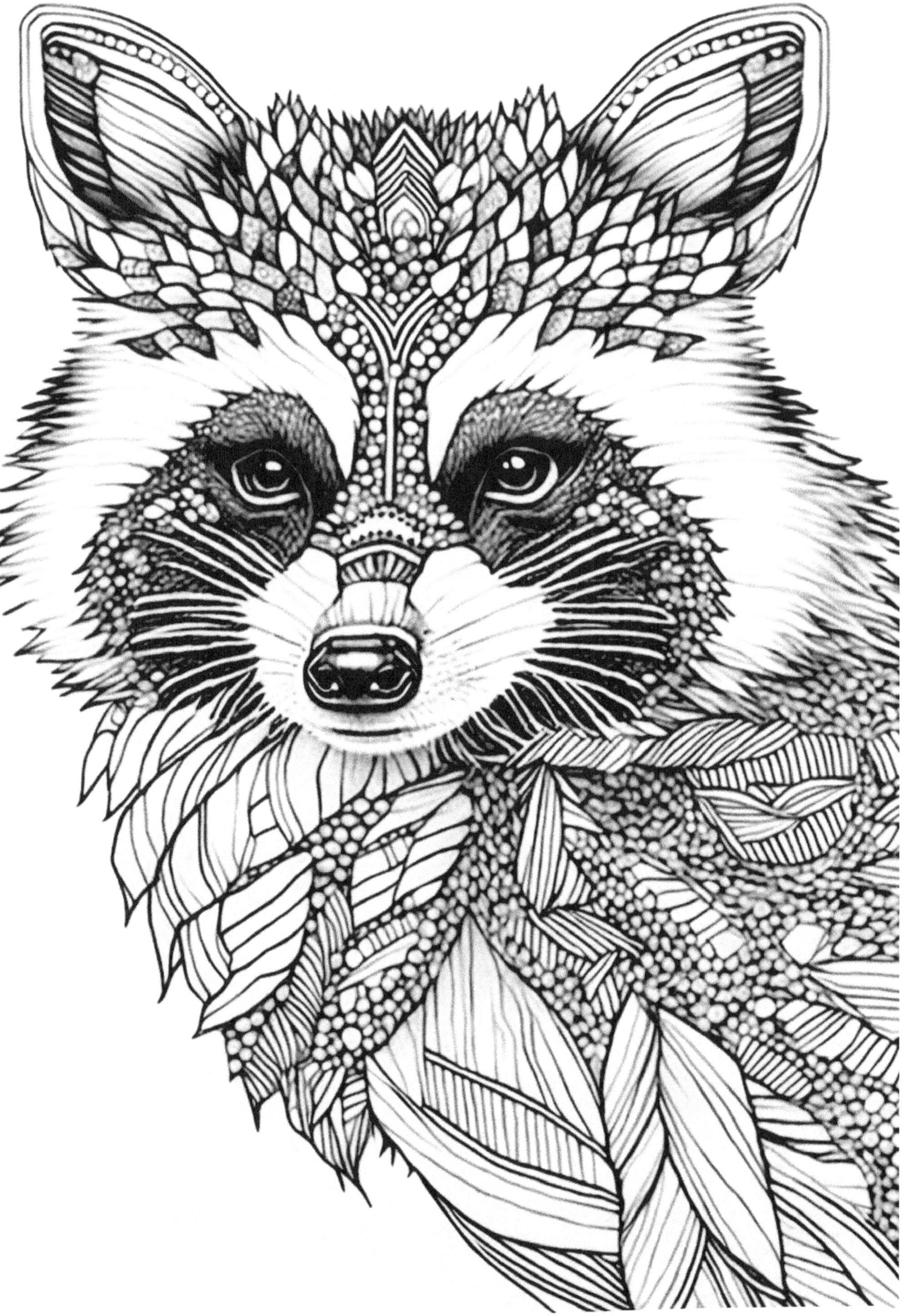

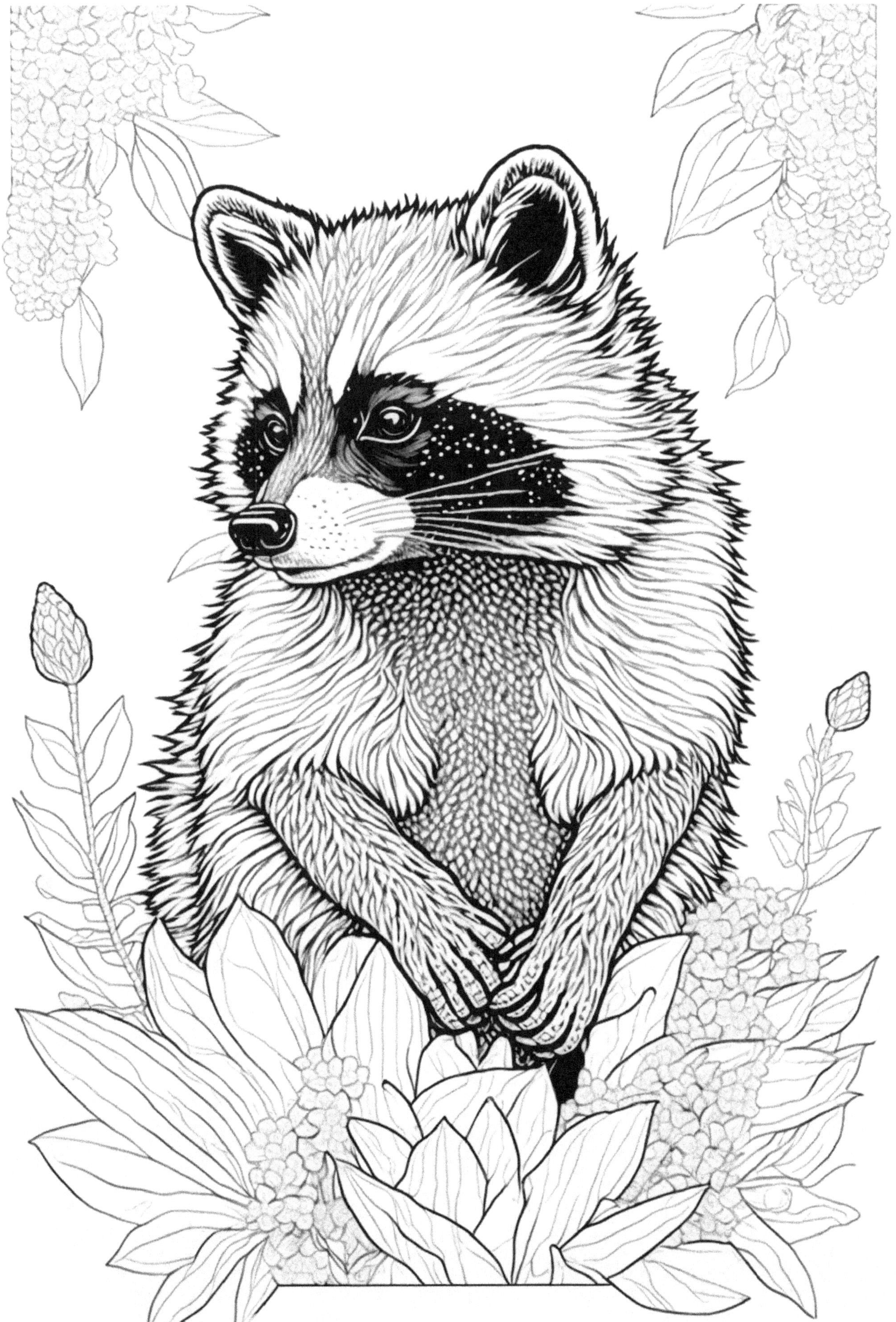

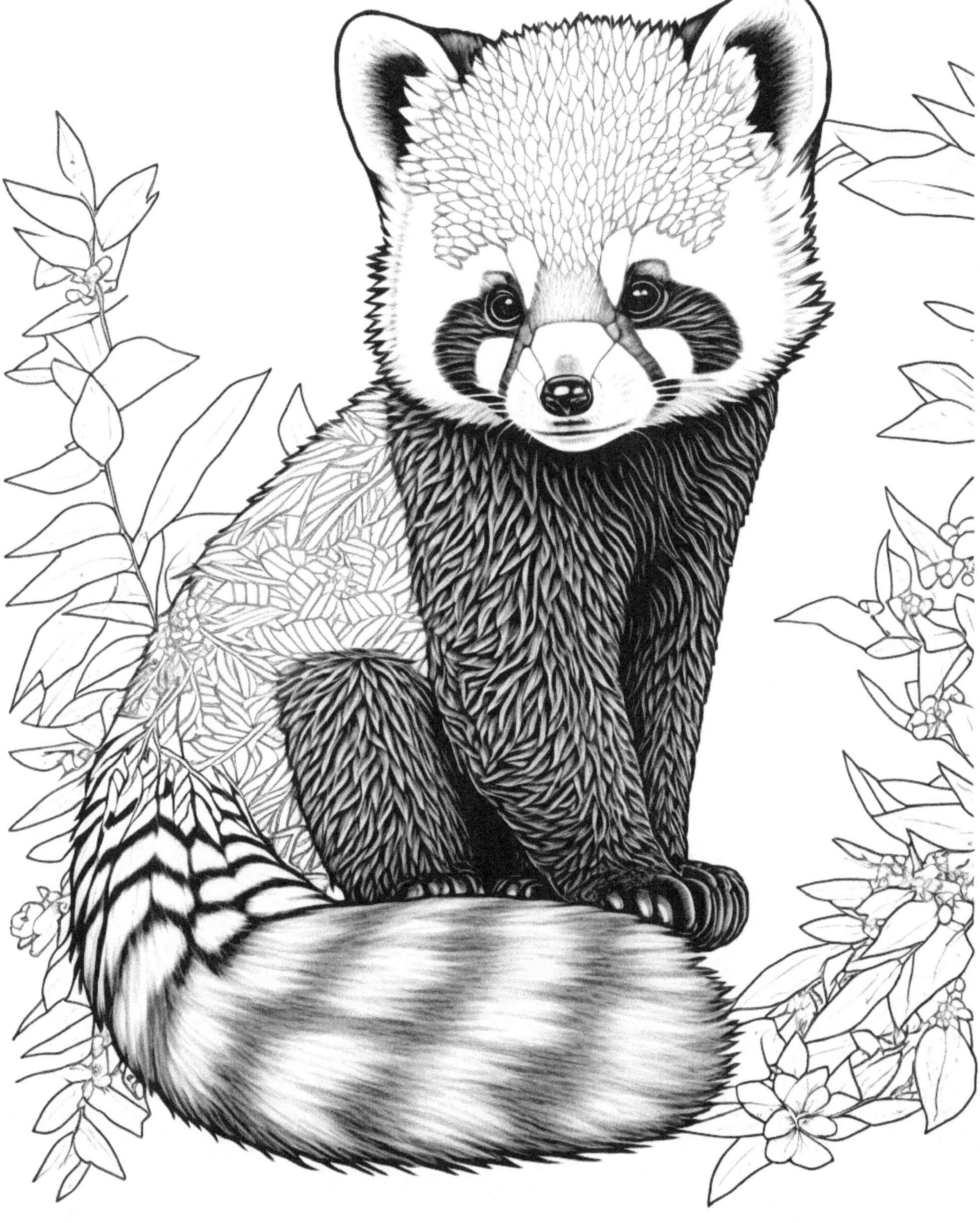

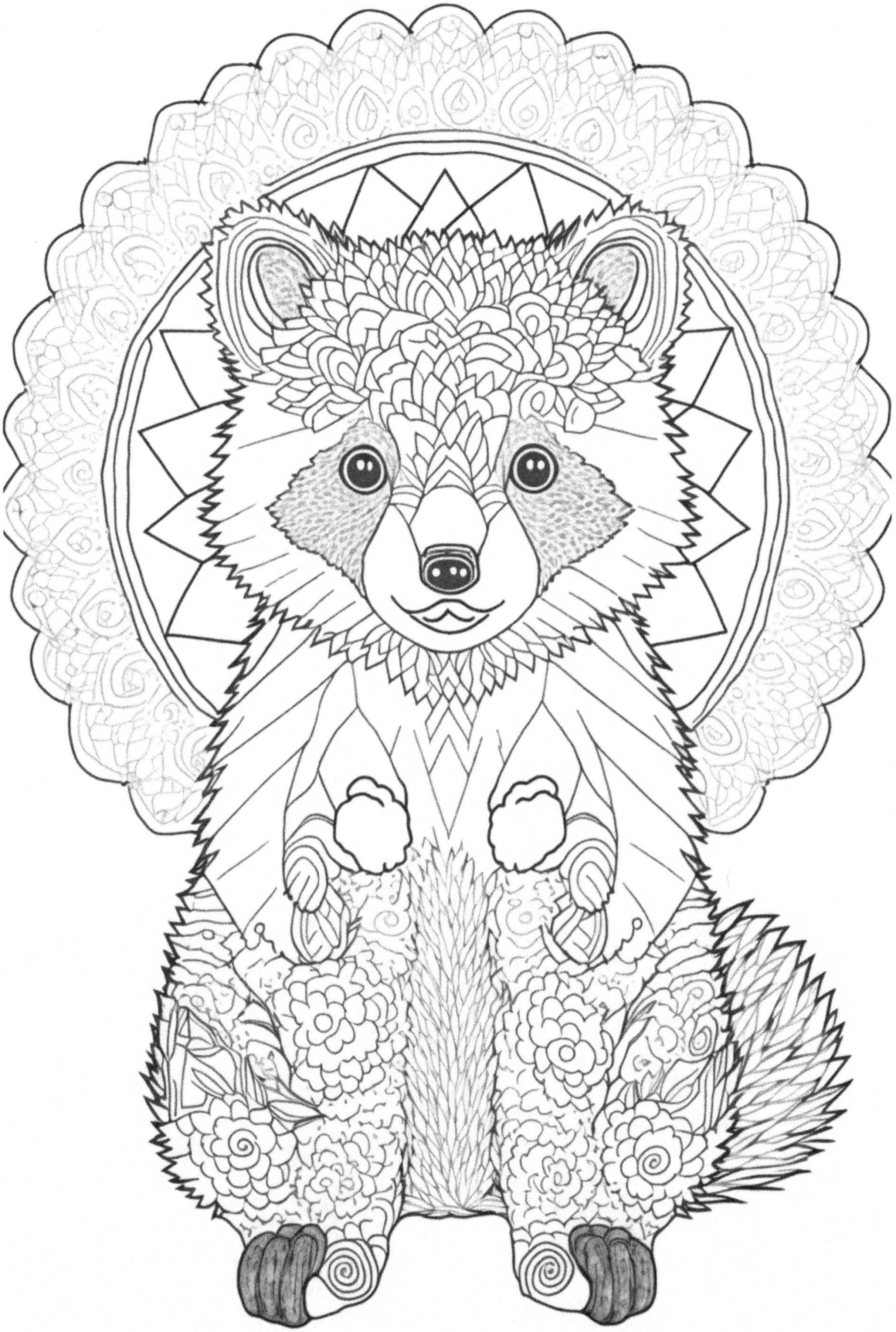

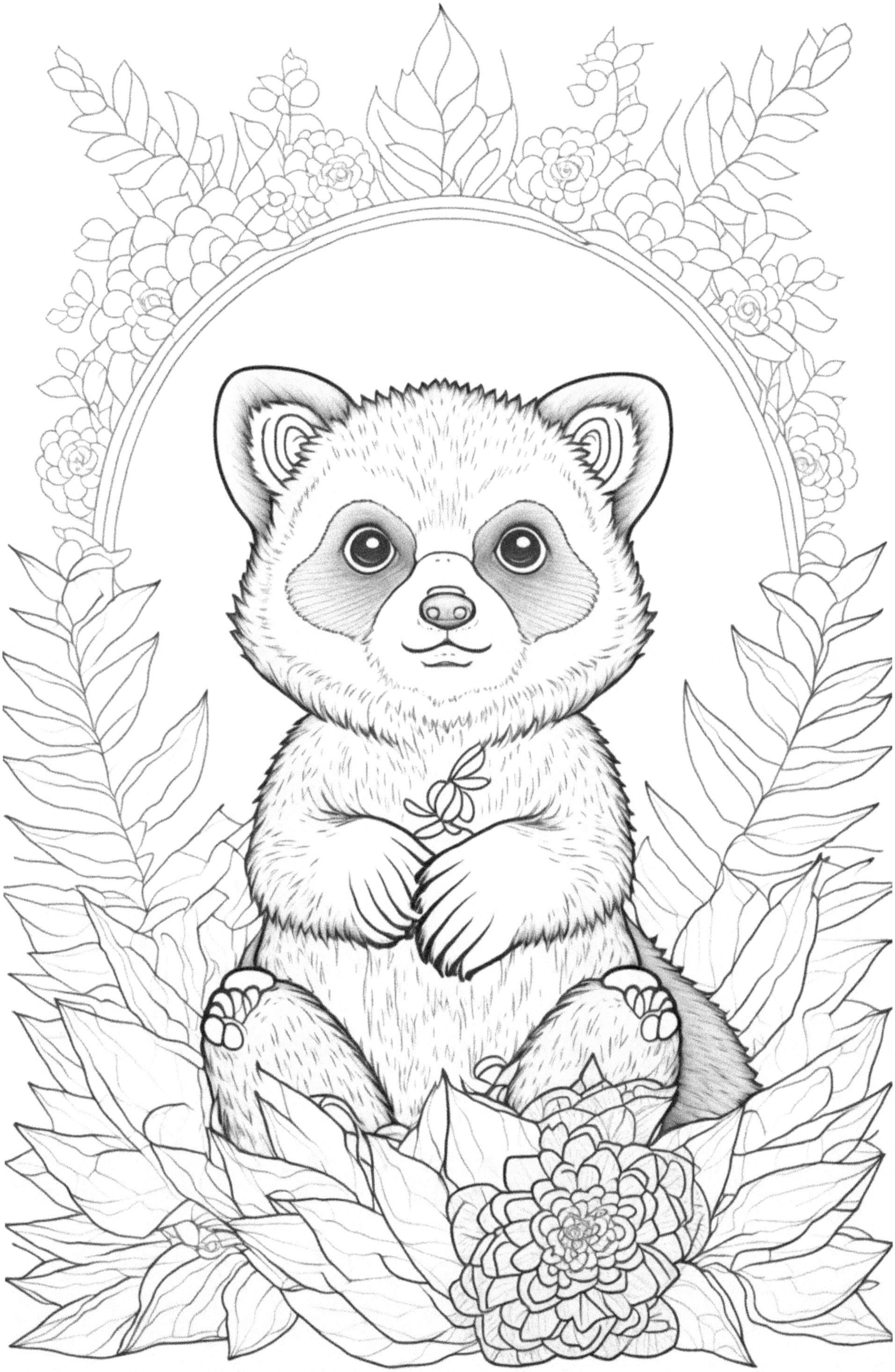

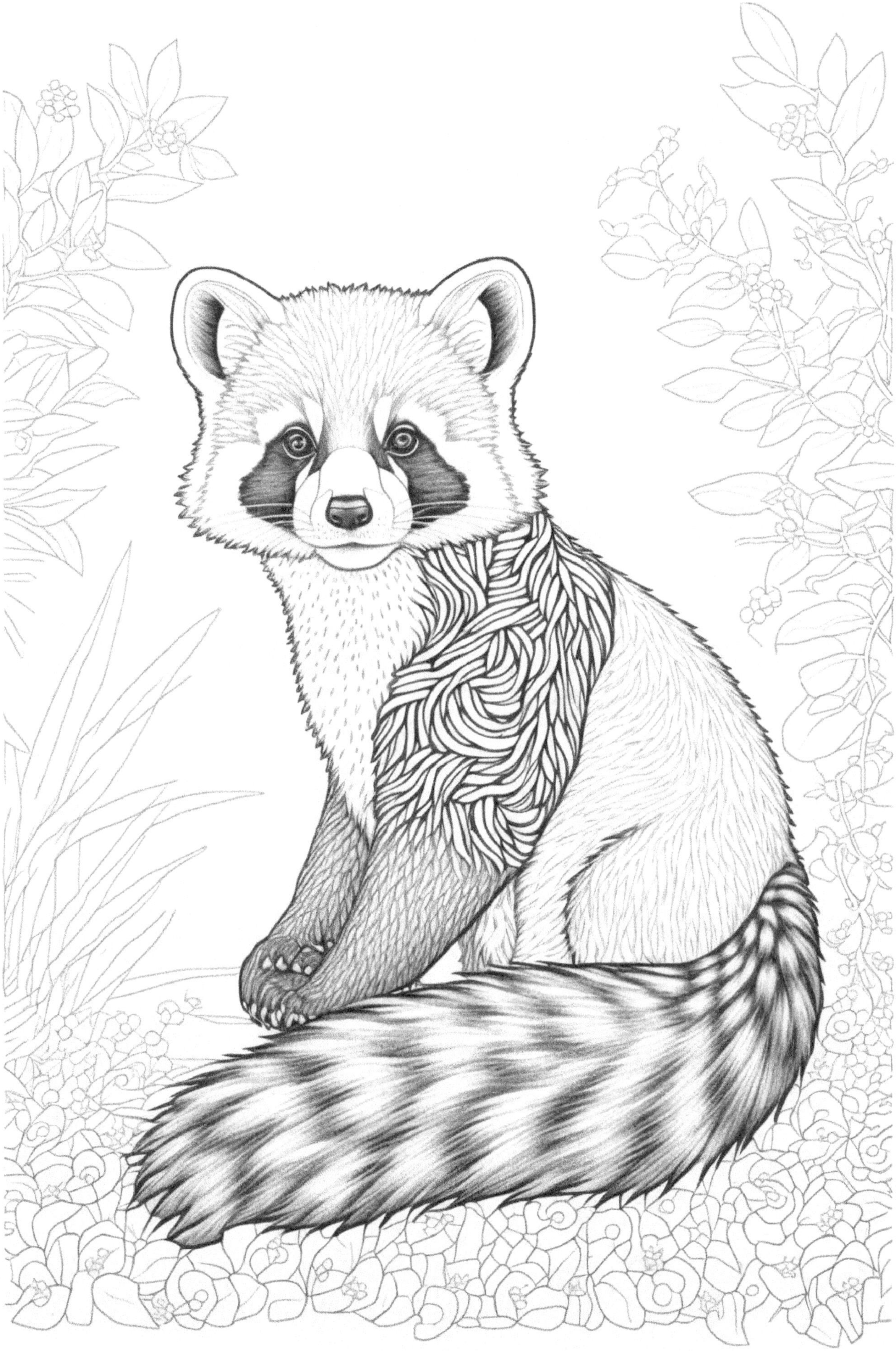

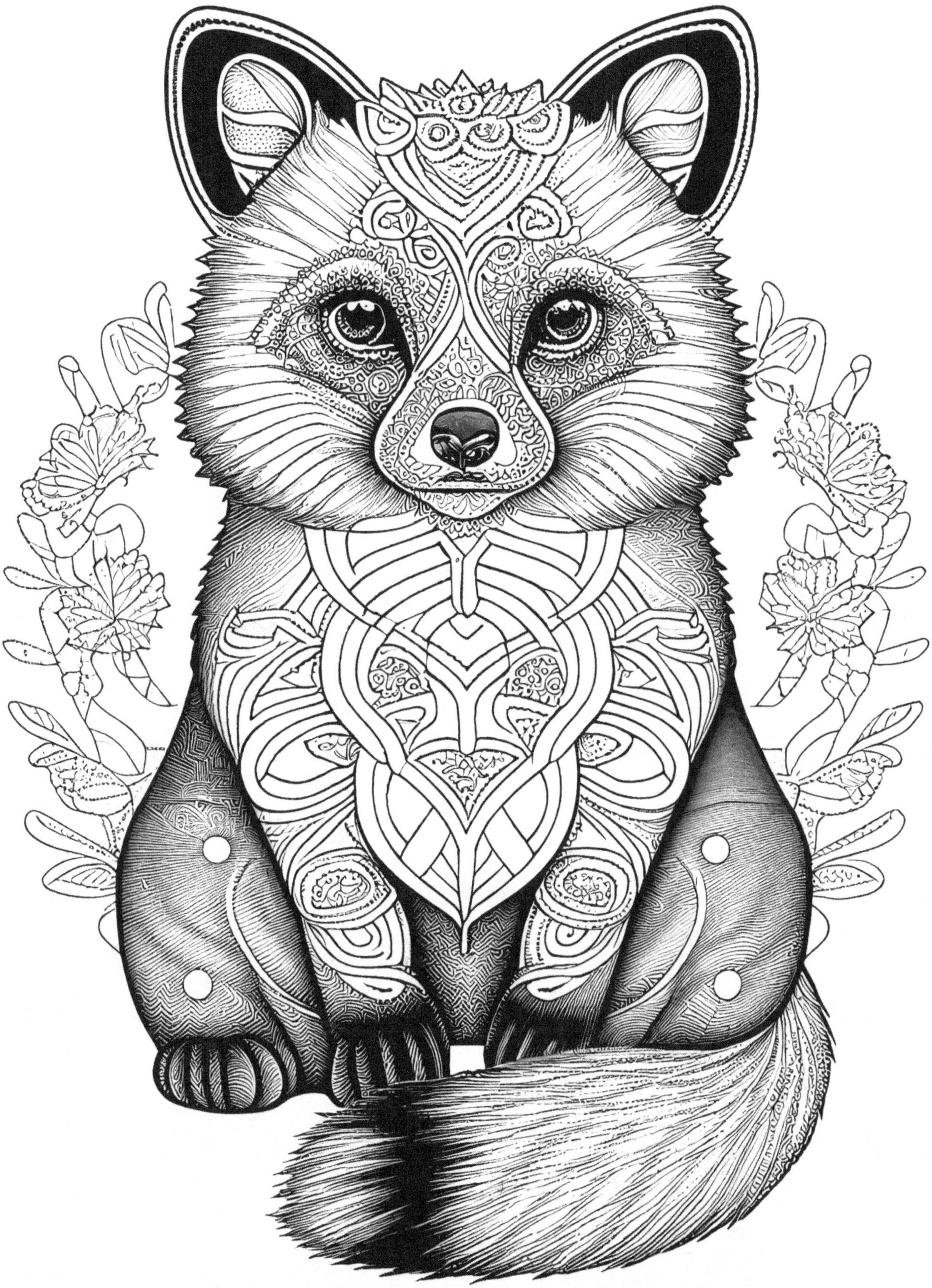

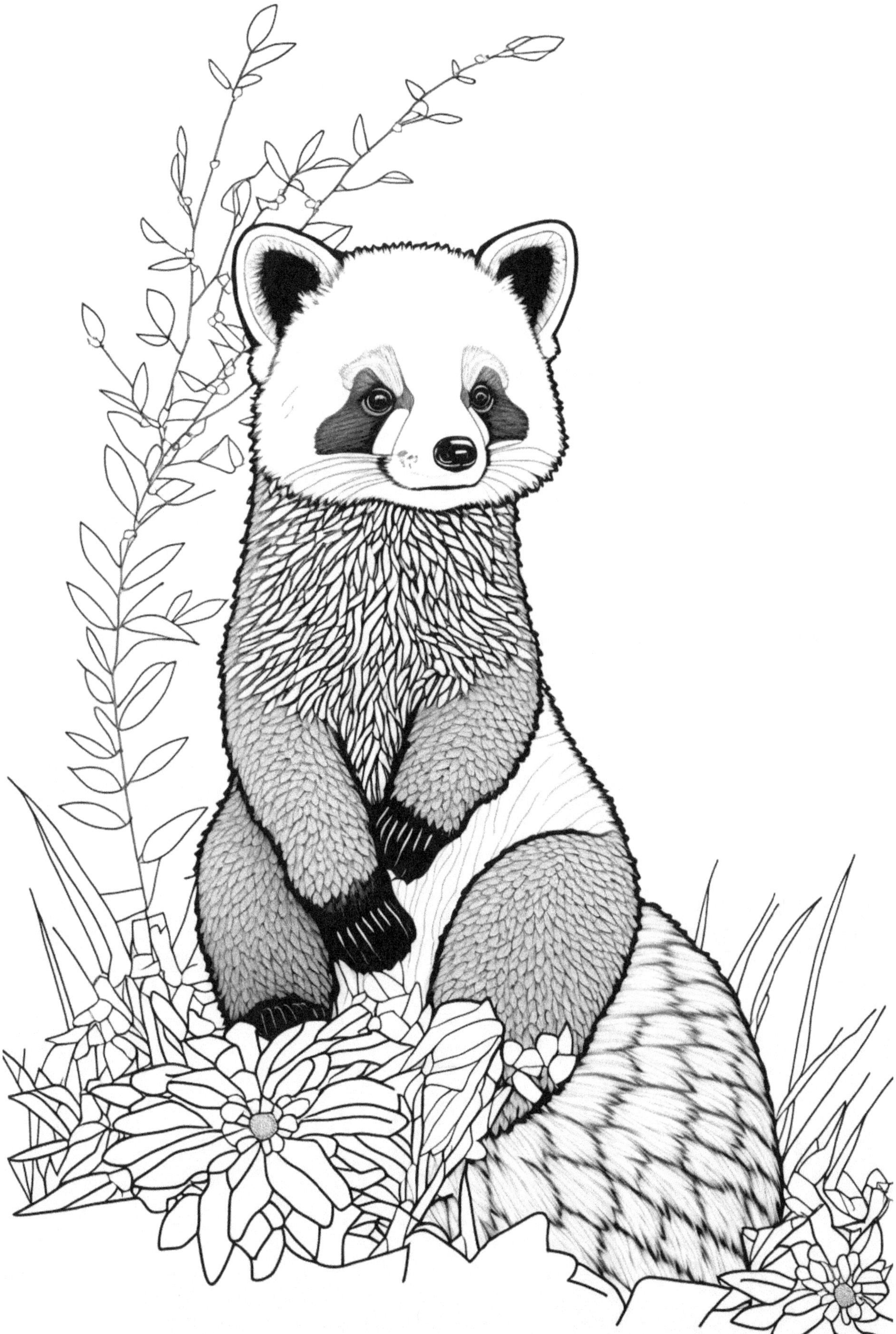

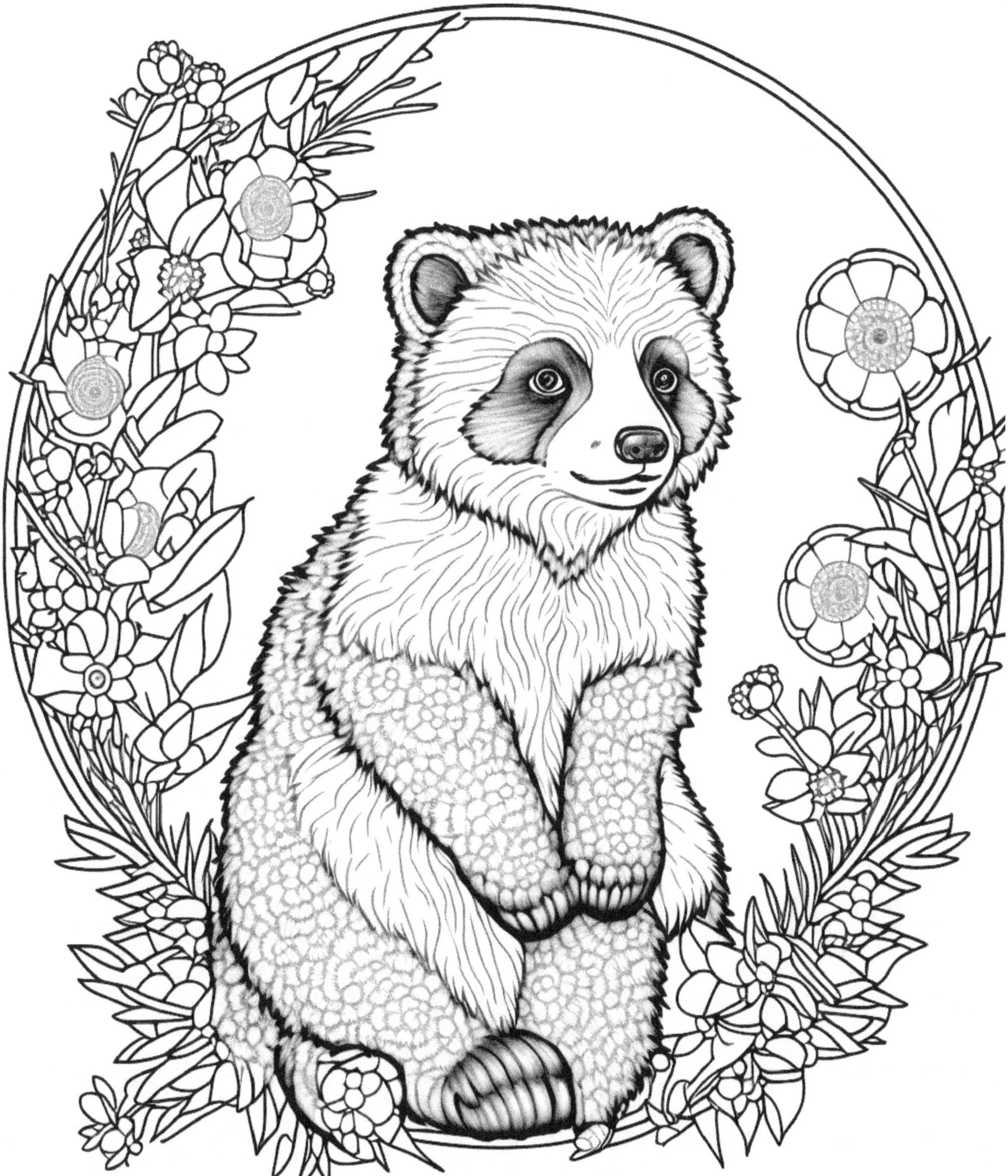

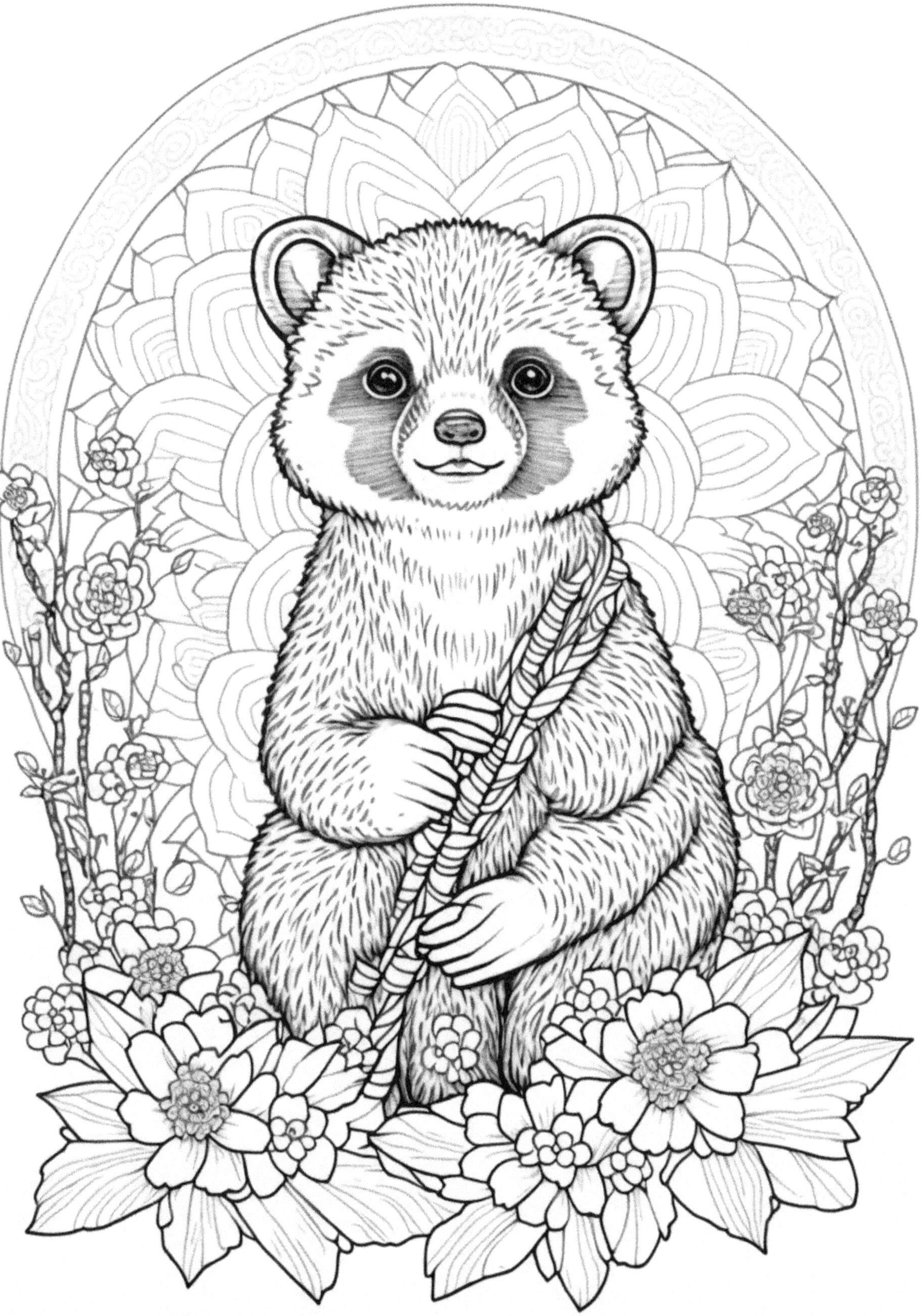

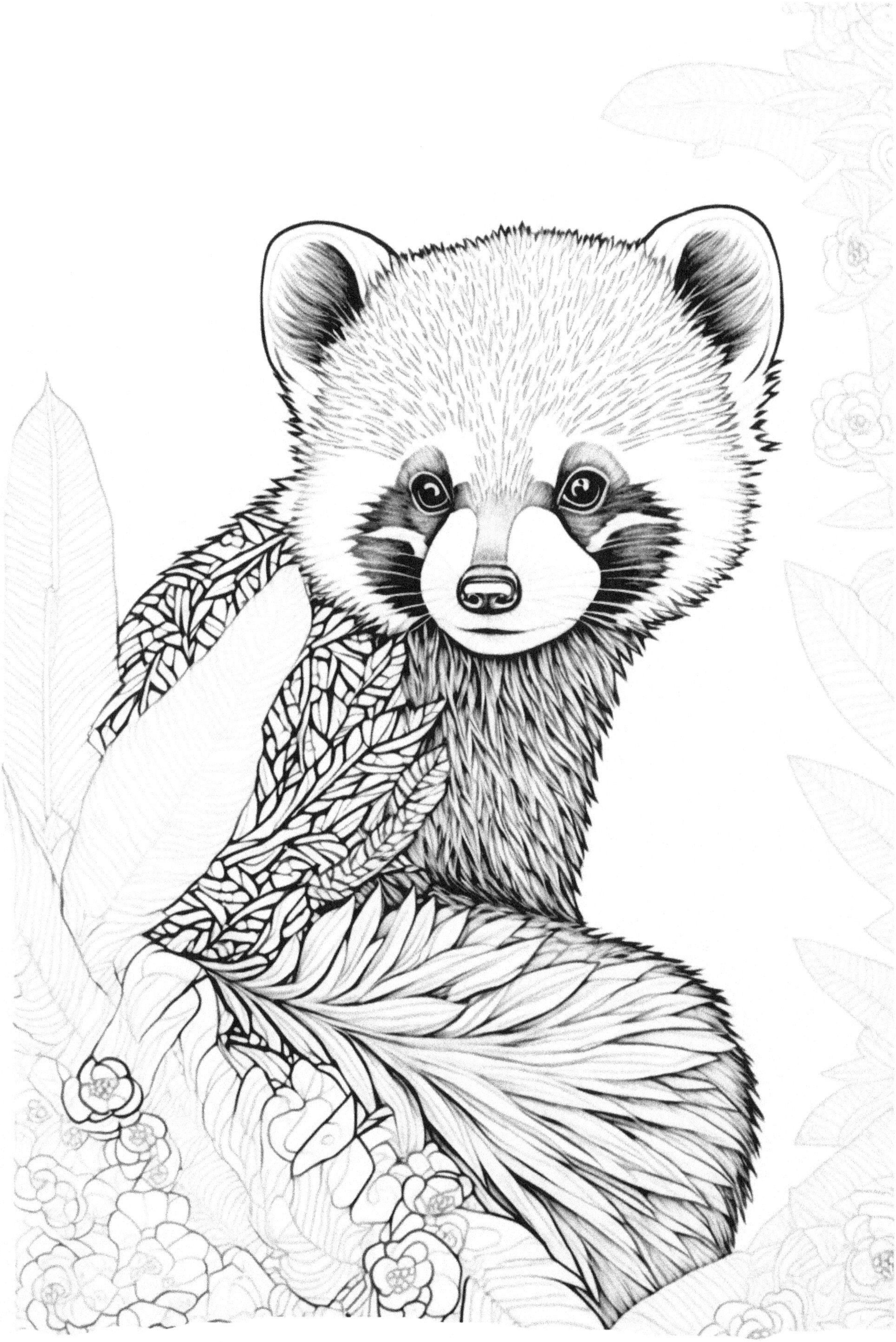

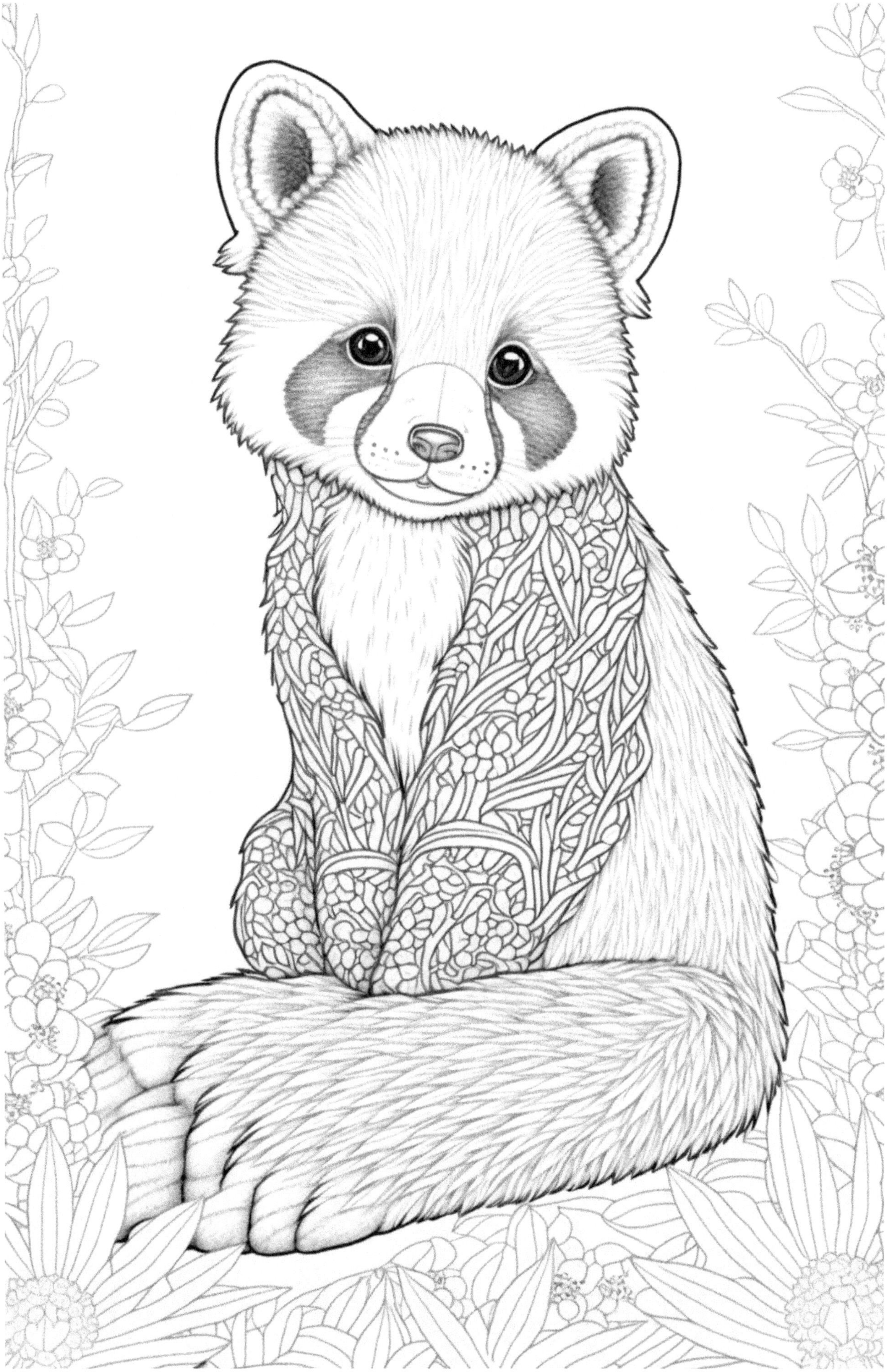

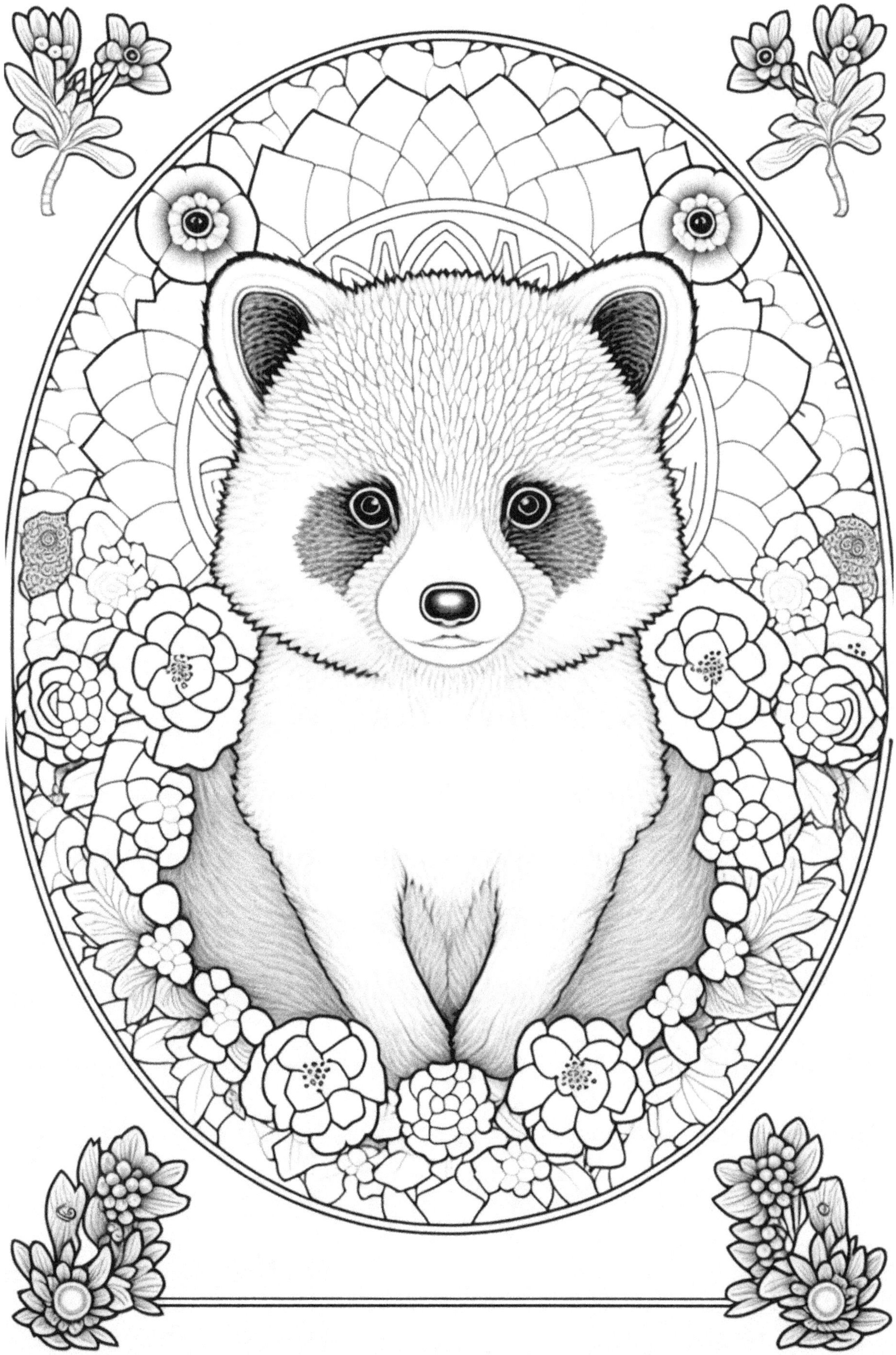

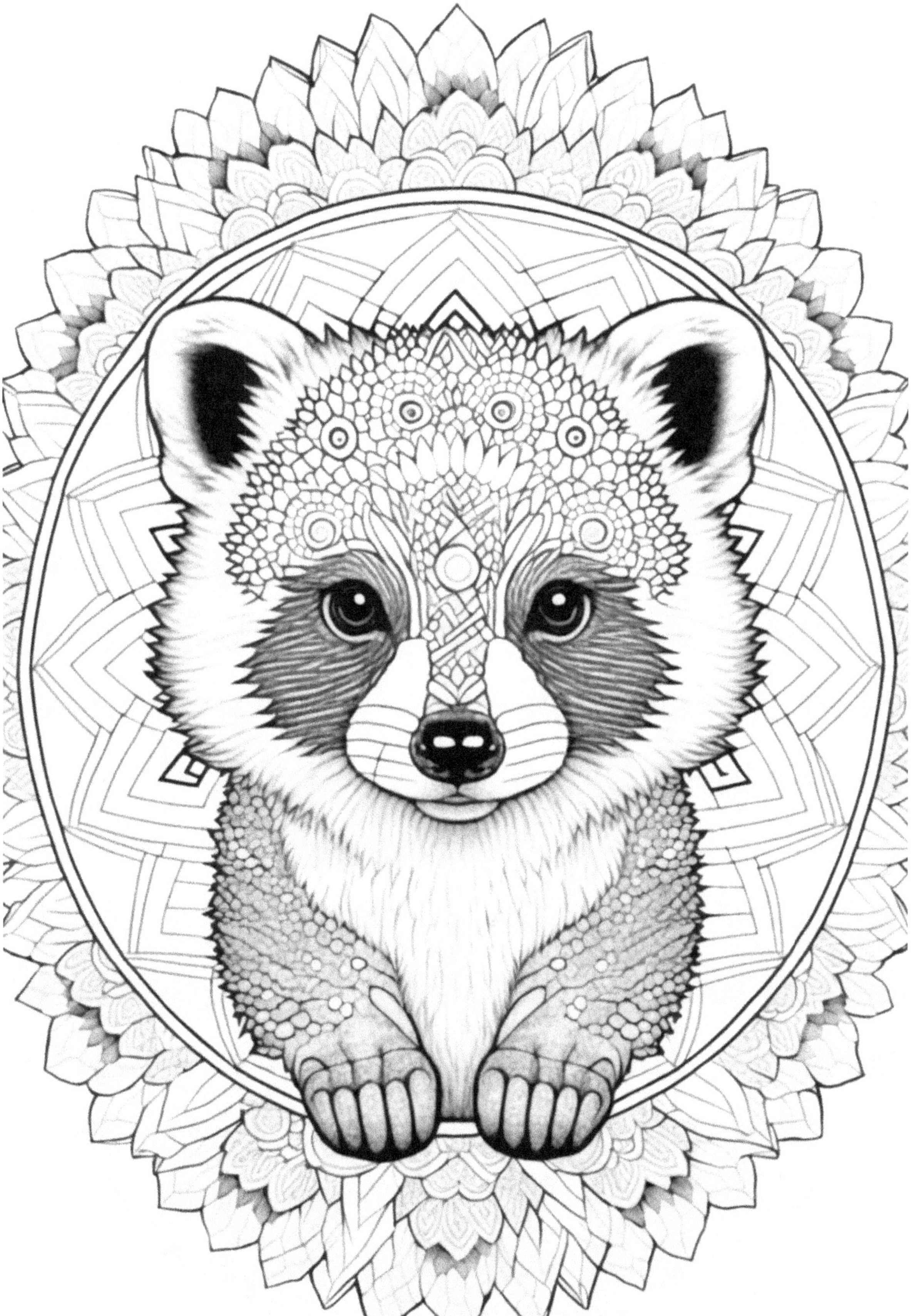

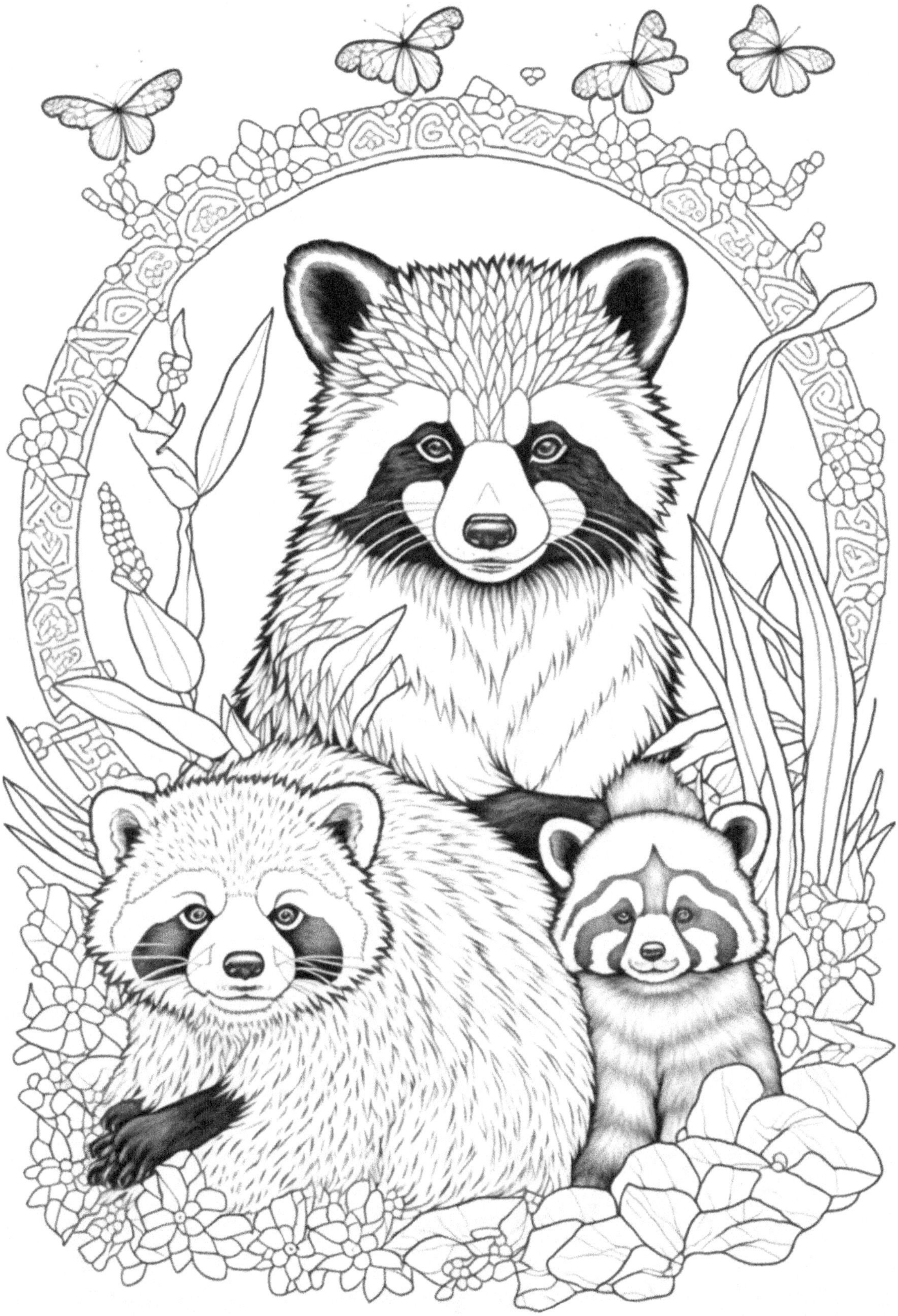

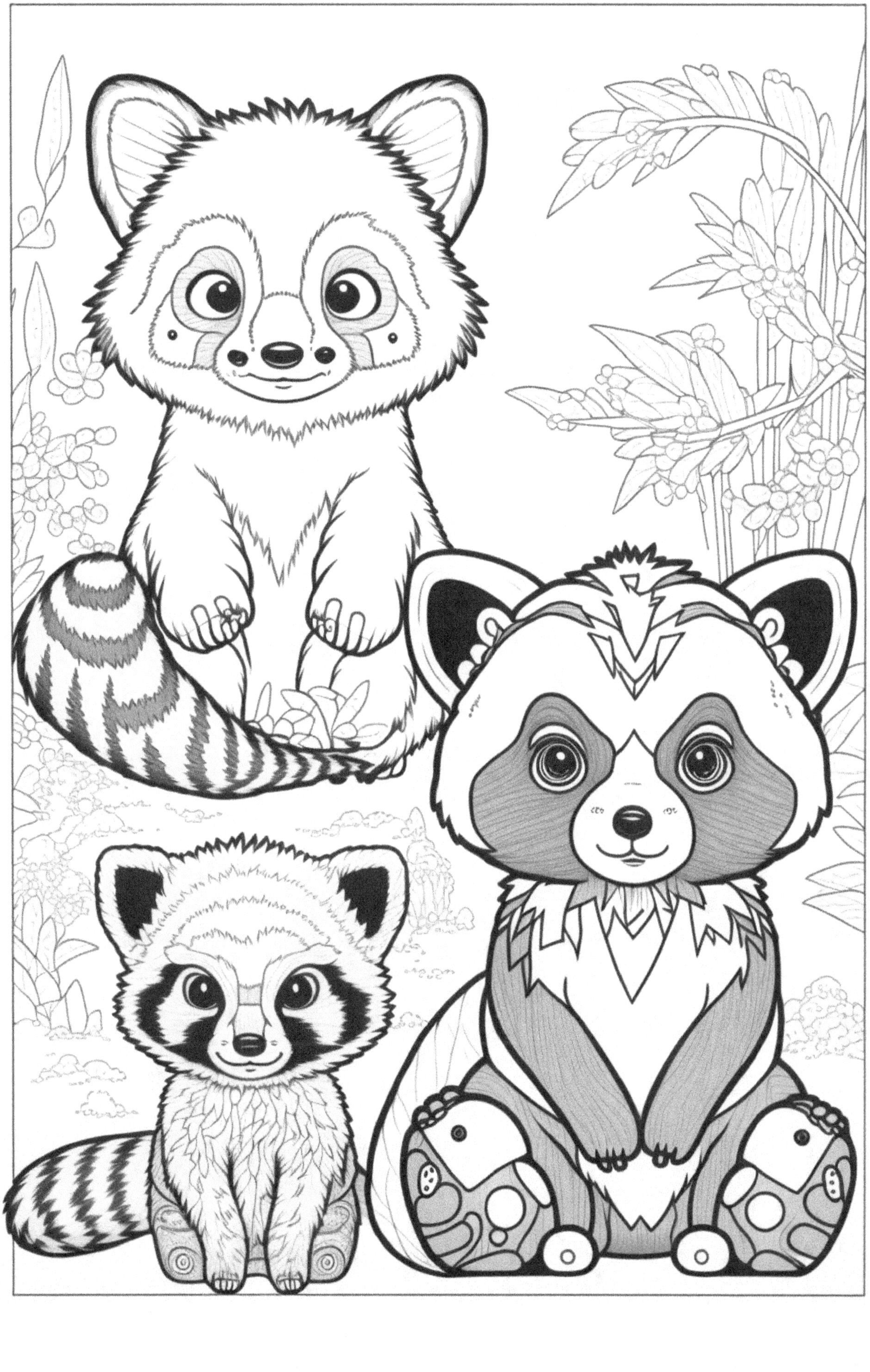

www.ingramcontent.com/pod-product-compliance
Lightning Source LLC
Chambersburg PA
CBHW082150230526
45467CB00043B/2755
9798389181335